POCKET MANUAL

ECO WARRIOR

'A new relationship that respects rather than exploits the wonders of nature must be created in the wake of the coronavirus pandemic.'

Sir David Attenborough

Published in October 2020

A catalogue record for this book is available from the British Library

ISBN 978 1 78521 725 8

Library of Congress Control Number: 2020932617

Design and layout by Richard Parsons

Published by J H Haynes & Co. Ltd.,
Sparkford, Yeovil, Somerset BA22 7JJ, UK
Tel: 01963 440635, Int. tel: +44 1963 440635
Website: www.haynes.com

Haynes North America Inc.,
859 Lawrence Drive, Newbury Park, California 91320, USA

Printed in Malaysia

With thanks to WWF climate specialist Shirley Matheson for expert advice and comment.

With thanks to Alamy for use of the following images: pp7, 11 left, 16, 22, 23, 29, 44, 47 top, 48, 50, 51 top, 57, 58, 62, 67, 69, 106, 117 top.

The Author

Catherine Barr studied ecology before campaigning with Greenpeace for many years on wildlife and trade issues. She then trained as a journalist and worked for the Natural History Museum in London, working with scientists to write and edit exhibitions. Since 2005, she has been writing non-fiction picture books to spark interest and encourage action to protect the natural world.
Twitter: @catherine_barr/Instagram: @catherinebarrbooks

POCKET MANUAL
ECO
WARRIOR

ECO WARRIOR
CONTENTS

INTRODUCTION

All life on Earth relies on the natural world to survive. We depend on nature for our health, food and most of our medicines. We need thriving ecosystems and abundant natural resources for our homes and modern lives. But humans have become greedy.

Our species, *Homo sapiens*, means 'wise man'. But we are not always wise. We are taking a lot more from nature than we need, and we are knowingly causing climate change. This is threatening

'We showed that we are united and that we, young people, are unstoppable.'
Greta Thunberg, UN Youth Climate Summit, New York City, 21 September 2019

WHAT IS AN ECO WARRIOR?

An activist who helps to stop damage to the environment and raises awareness of the problems *and* solutions so other people join in to help.

the survival of all life on Earth. For the first time, just one species – humanity – is having a massive impact on the planet. There are now 7.7 billion people on Earth. For this reason, many scientists call this geological period the Anthropocene, or the Age of Humans.

We humans have the knowledge and understanding to stop climate change, and to live wisely and sustainably, in harmony with nature. We have discovered and rediscovered better ways of making energy, growing food and finding technological solutions that will help us care for the world's natural resources and protect global biodiversity.

There is enough space, enough water and enough natural resources for all life on Earth to thrive. If we share what we need and share the stories of success, together we can save planet Earth.

That's exactly what eco warriors do… Want to be one?

Yes? Let's get started. The first step is to explore 'some' of the big issues and find out what really inspires you to get involved!

THE BIG ISSUES

Dip in to discover what will inspire you to become an eco warrior ... what makes you curious or sparks interest, wonder, passion or outrage?

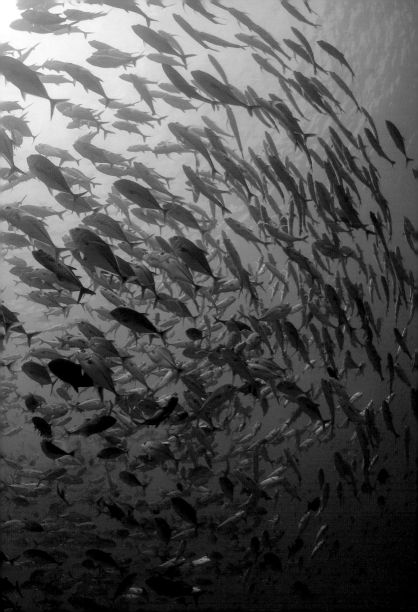

CLIMATE CHANGE

The climate has changed many times since Earth was formed 4.5 billion years ago but this time human activities and the way we live our lives are causing the climate to change faster than ever before. Climate change means that the temperatures and weather patterns on Earth are changing. This is upsetting the balance of nature and threatening life on land and in the sea in lots of different ways.

'We really need to kick the carbon habit and stop making our energy from burning things. Climate change is also really important. You can wreck one rainforest then move, drain one area of resources and move onto another, but climate change is global.'

Sir David Attenborough, natural historian

'We are running the most dangerous experiment in history right now, which is to see how much carbon dioxide the atmosphere can handle before there is an environmental catastrophe.'
Elon Musk, CEO of Tesla and SpaceX

DID YOU KNOW?

The Intergovernmental Panel on Climate Change says that scientific evidence for warming of the climate system is unequivocal. Go to www.climate.nasa.gov/evidence to find out more.

WHAT CAUSES IT?

Climate change is caused by increased levels of so-called 'greenhouse gases' in the troposphere. These gases build up in our atmosphere and stop heat escaping from the Earth, so it warms up. The more greenhouse gases there are, the thicker the 'blanket' of gases is around the planet. Two of the most powerful greenhouse gases are carbon dioxide and methane.

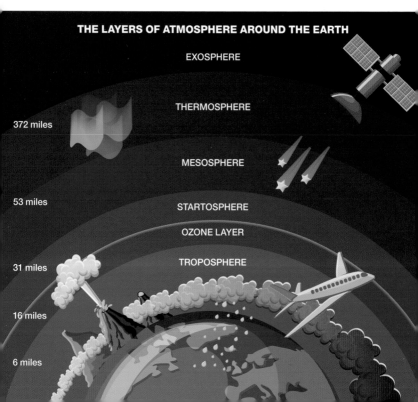

THE LAYERS OF ATMOSPHERE AROUND THE EARTH

EXOSPHERE

THERMOSPHERE

372 miles

MESOSPHERE

53 miles

STARTOSPHERE

OZONE LAYER

31 miles TROPOSPHERE

16 miles

6 miles

Two causes of climate change are burning fossil fuels, and intensive cattle farming.

Fossil fuels

By burning fossil fuels – oil, coal and gas – to make energy to drive cars, fly planes, fuel machines and heat homes, humans are adding increasing amounts of carbon dioxide to the air.

Intensive farming

Large-scale, intensive farming adds to climate change because when cows (and sheep) fart and burp they release methane. Cattle farming, particularly in the Amazon, is causing massive deforestation as trees are cleared to make space for fields. Deforestation makes climate change worse because forests absorb carbon dioxide in the air during the day and store the carbon for many years. When trees are cut down, this carbon is released back into the atmosphere. Deforested land can't absorb carbon dioxide from the atmosphere.

So, when we cut down trees for farming, we lose an important natural climate solution to reducing carbon dioxide in the air and at the same time increase the greenhouse gases. Both of these things accelerate climate change.

WHAT HAPPENS?

Climate change is affecting ecosystems that animals and people rely on for shelter and food. It is forcing animals and people to move to safer places to live. Animals that can't adapt to a new environment or move quickly enough are becoming extinct. This is one reason why our planet is experiencing an extinction event, also known as a 'mass extinction'.

The global warming caused by climate change is also melting polar ice caps and glaciers. The meltwater is causing higher sea levels, which threaten low-lying islands. If this continues, these rising seas will threaten homes and even major coastal cities, such as New York, Beijing and London.

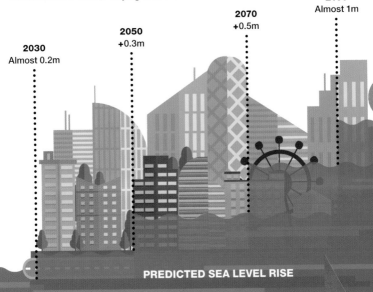

2030
Almost 0.2m

2050
+0.3m

2070
+0.5m

2100
Almost 1m

PREDICTED SEA LEVEL RISE

The Paris Agreement

This is an international climate change pact that was adopted in Paris on 12 December 2015. Countries from around the world made an important agreement to speed up action to tackle climate change together. So far, 197 countries have signed up, but the USA, one of the world's biggest climate polluters, is pulling out, rejecting this historic opportunity to fight climate change.

Parliament, Brussels, Belgium, November 2018

Altiero Spinelli

In addition to rising seas, climate change is causing more frequent and more extreme weather, such as hurricanes and floods. Weather patterns are becoming less predictable, too. This means, for example, that in many parts of the world farmers can no longer rely on regular rains to water their crops.

Top scientists around the world are trying to understand the effects better. They are projecting how the climate will change over time and some of the effects that we will see.

FOOD PRODUCTION

Intensive livestock farming, mostly cattle farming for beef, has a huge effect on the planet. According to the latest science, an important way to reduce your environmental impact on Earth is to avoid meat and dairy – animal products such as milk and cheese. People can help to reduce their carbon footprint by eating a more plant-based diet. However, it is important to eat a balanced diet to get all the nutrients and protein you need.

DID YOU KNOW?

Food miles is the distance that an item of food travels from the place where it was produced to the place it is eaten. These journeys are usually powered by fossil fuels, which adds to climate change.

Challenges

To feed the world in a sustainable way:
Think about what you choose to eat by eating food that has been sustainably farmed or fished.

Cut down on meat:
Reduce the amount of red meat (beef and lamb) that you eat. From meat-free burgers to tofu, pulses and beans, there are lots of alternative proteins to meat.

Improve animal welfare:
Intensive farming to raise cheaper food means that animals, including fish, live in crowded and often cruel conditions. These factory farms increase the risk of disease to animals and people, as they may have high levels of medicines like antibiotics.

Intensive farming

The climate impact of meat production is big because intensive cattle farming:

- Results in massive deforestation when large areas of rainforests are cut down to make space for cattle to graze.
- Requires a huge amount of fresh water – in fact, 85 per cent of all the fresh water on the planet is used in agriculture.
- Creates climate change emissions – carbon dioxide is released when forest is burned to create farmland; and methane, a powerful greenhouse gas, is released by cows and other chewing livestock like sheep.

Overfishing

Taking too many fish from the oceans is destroying the marine environment and threatening future fish stocks. Tragically dolphins, whales and turtles are often caught in nets by mistake. This 'bycatch' is threatening the survival of many marine species.

Looking ahead

A 'planetary health diet' contains less red meat and sugar and is packed with lots of vegetables, pulses, fruits, seeds and nuts. If you tuck into a plate of food more like this you will limit climate change, boost your health and help protect the planet.

DISCOVER MORE

The planetary health diet suggests a more plant-based diet with less meat and dairy.
www.eatforum.org

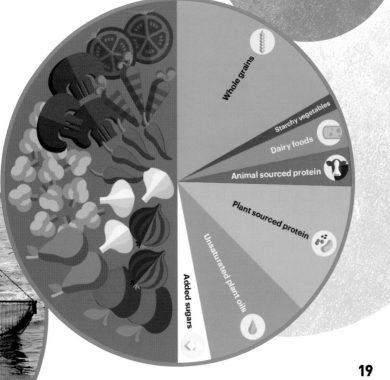

Whole grains

Starchy vegetables

Dairy foods

Animal sourced protein

Plant sourced protein

Unsaturated plant oils

Added sugars

THE BIG ISSUES
HABITATS

The natural places where every form of life on Earth – including people – find food, water, shelter, homes and mates are called habitats. From hot desert to lush rainforest and the frozen poles, habitats are all the wildly different places where animals and plants live.

DID YOU KNOW?

There are eight different types of habitat: Oceans, Rivers and lakes, Forests, Grasslands, Hot deserts, Polar ice, Mountain and Tundra.

Challenges

Rising human population:

As the number of people on Earth grows, humans are taking up more space on land, damaging habitats like forests and polluting the oceans and unique habitats like mangroves. People are using more natural resources, such as timber, water, oil and minerals, and habitats are being destroyed to make space for farms and cities. As habitats become damaged, polluted and disappear, animals are becoming extinct and there is growing conflict between people and wildlife.

Climate change:

As global weather patterns change, important habitats such as coral reefs are dying and others are changing. This is forcing animals and people to move to find new and safer places to live as flooding, drought and rising, warming seas destroy their homes and threaten their food suplies.

What is a protected area?

These are places where people are looking after nature for the benefit of wildlife and humans. This means that any human activities in these places must be sustainable – they cannot damage the environment in the long term.

What is a rewilding?

The large-scale restoration of ecosystems where nature can take care of itself. It encourages a balance between people and the rest of nature, meaning that each can thrive.

DISCOVER MORE

In Ennerdale Valley in the Lake District, nature is being allowed to take control... mixed forest is replacing dark conifer forest, sheep numbers are reduced and the Marsh Fritillary butterfly has been introduced: rewildlingbritain.org

'Only a quarter of all land is substantially free from human activities.'
WWF Living Planet Report, 2018

Looking ahead

Around the world, wilderness is disappearing. This particularly affects nature's big predators, such as wolves, bears, tigers and lions, which play an important role at the top of the food chain, keeping nature in balance. Rewilding is reintroducing some of these animals, helping to recreate well-balanced ecosystems that are more able to cope with the impact of climate change.

Like all animals, we depend on the natural world to survive. If we respect rather than damage or pollute nature when we build our homes, and fish, farm and grow our food, we benefit from sharing the environment with other life on Earth.

Fifteen per cent of the land on Earth is protected in national parks and other areas, but less than 6 per cent of the oceans are protected areas. It is vital to manage these protected areas well, so that they provide clean water, food, shelter and protection for people from natural disasters like floods.

DISCOVER MORE

Yellowstone National Park has been restored by the rewilding of wolves... bears, beavers, riverside tree species and song birds have returned to this wilderness previously overgrazed by elk: yellowstonepark.com

BIODIVERSITY

The term 'biodiversity' refers to the variety of life on Earth – the different plants, fungi, animals and microorganisms that have evolved from our common ancestor in the deep ocean 3.8 million years ago. Scientists think there are 1.5 million species on Earth. But for the first time in Earth's history, the actions of one species, humans are driving huge numbers of plants and animals to extinction.

ATMOSPHERE (AIR)

BIOSPHERE

HYDROSPHERE (WATER) LITHOSPHERE (EARTH)

'We want to see a world where wildlife trade is sustainably managed, maintains healthy populations, contributes to development and helps motivate commitments to conserve wild species and habitats.'
Steven Broad, TRAFFIC, wildlife trade specialists

The big drivers

Alongside climate change, the biggest causes of biodiversity decline are over-exploitation of wildlife, and habitat loss on land and in the oceans. These actions threaten wild animals but they also threaten our own survival.

Shy scaly mammals called pangolins are the most traded animal in the world, for their scales and meat.

There has been, for example, a dramatic reduction in the number of bees and other pollinators, which we rely on for the production of our food and biodiversity in wild places. Deforestation, meanwhile, makes flooding more likely.

The wildlife trade

The human population is growing fast, and around the world we use thousands of species every day for food and medicine. This over-exploitation is unsustainable. As many as 10,000 species are going extinct every year. This biodiversity crisis is now the 6th mass extinction on Earth (the 5th was the extinction of the dinosaurs), but this one is caused by our activity on the planet: hunting, fishing, logging, and reducing or polluting natural habitats. The cruel and illegal wildlife trade in elephant ivory, tigers, pangolins as well as many lesser known animals and plants like rosewood trees, threatens to wipe out some of the most iconic creatures on the planet... all of which play a critical role in the ecosystems where they live.

The IUCN Red List

Red signals danger and this global red list of 116,000 plants, animals and fungi includes many that face the danger of extinction. The IUCN Red List is a giant database collated by over 8,000 scientists around the world, of information about biodiversity on Earth. The information on this red list is used to help make conservation plans to protect vulnerable, threatened and endangered species. More than 31,000 species on the list are threatened with extinction.

IUCN RED LIST

Check out the
IUCN Red List of
AMAZING SPECIES:
www.iucnredlist.org

'Species population declines are especially pronounced in the tropics... Freshwater species numbers have also declined dramatically... There has been a 60 per cent fall in biodiversity in just 40 years.'
WWF Living Planet Report, 2018

Looking ahead

We need biodiversity on Earth. Apart from its stunning beauty, amazing complexity and eye-popping wonder, all life depends on other life to survive. So we need to work harder to protect and restore that biodiversity. There are millions of species that scientists have not yet discovered, especially in the rainforest and in the deep oceans. These may include plants and animals that can help us cure diseases and work out how to survive in extreme environments on Earth, and even on Mars!

FRESH WATER

All water on Earth comes from rain. It is renewable, recycled endlessly between the Earth and the air in the global water cycle. Most rain becomes salty seawater as it runs over rocks into the oceans. Just 3 per cent of all the planet's water is fresh water, and most of this is locked in glacial ice at the poles. The tiny proportion of remaining liquid fresh water flows in lakes and rivers on land, or in huge aquifers underground. As the number of people on Earth rises, we are using more water and our stores above and below ground are running low.

DID YOU KNOW?

1 in 3 people globally do not have access to fresh water according to UNICEF and the World Health Organization 2019.

Challenges

People are grabbing and polluting water:

Some people in the world use lots of water and others, mostly people in poor countries, use less. Often, their water supplies are dirty and polluted. Without clean water to drink and wash with, millions of people are dying from waterborne diseases.

Most fresh water is used for farming:

About 85 per cent of the world's fresh water is used for agriculture. This is mostly livestock agriculture, though a huge amount of water is also required for cotton and sugar production. Irrigation systems to water crops have existed since ancient times but today, bigger and bigger farms are grabbing water, leaving others without it.

Unreliable rainfall:

Climate change means that weather all over the world is becoming less reliable and more extreme. Sometimes it floods and crops are washed away, and sometimes it doesn't rain at all. Both of these mean that many farmers are struggling to grow crops to feed their families or to sell to feed the rest of the world.

Water shortage and water pollution are growing global problems. Around the world people use 10 billion tons of fresh water every day.

'Contaminated water can transmit diseases such as diarrhoea, cholera, dysentery, typhoid, and polio. Contaminated drinking water is estimated to cause 485,000 diarrhoeal deaths each year.'
World Health Organization, June 2019

Looking ahead

Everyone on Earth has a right to clean, fresh water, so this precious resource must be shared wisely and carefully. If we did this, it would mean an end to people having to walk for many hours each day, only to collect a trickle of polluted water. Since most of the world's farmers are women in poor countries and it is mostly women and girls who must walk for hours each day to collect water, many girls do not have enough time to go to school, so the education of girls is closely linked to the problems of limited fresh water.

DISCOVER MORE

Access to safe water, for example a clean pump in a village, means more girls can go to school... this transforms their lives and their community.

THE BIG ISSUES
ENERGY

Most of the energy we use comes from burning fossil fuels: oil, coal and gas. These natural resources lie deep inside the Earth and were formed from decaying plants and animals millions of years ago. They are non-renewable, which means that one day they will run out.

Fossil fuels are burned to make energy to drive cars, fly aeroplanes, heat homes, cook food and power factories and schools. But there is a big problem … burning fossil fuels is driving climate change, which is now threatening life on Earth.

DID YOU KNOW?

Energy is the biggest source of greenhouse gases created by humans worldwide.

Challenges

Fossil fuels:

Burning fossil fuels releases carbon dioxide, one of the main drivers of climate change. The challenge is for clean renewable energy to be available and cheap enough for everyone to use so we can leave fossil fuels in the ground.

Power use:

A growing human population is using more and more energy to power modern life. However, the use of energy per person is very unequal across the world. People in richer countries use much more energy than people in poorer countries, where 1 billion people have no access to electricity at all.

Money:

Using fossil fuels is still cheaper and easier than using renewable energy in many countries because governments are still supporting the powerful fossil fuel industry, rather than prioritising renewable energy.

Energy types

Renewable energy is created by natural resources that are naturally replaced, such as the sun, water (called hydro electricity) wind, tides, waves and underground heat (called geothermal electricity). It is called clean, green energy because it does not pollute the air or water.

One of Costa Rica's hydroelectric power plants.

But there are challenges too. Dams that are built for hydroelectric energy production flood land, and disrupt river flow and fish migration. Costa Rica is set to be the first developing country in the world to be powered by 100% renewable energy, a mix of hydro, wind and geothermal energy.

Non-renewable energy is from sources that will run out in our lifetimes. Most non-renewable energy comes from fossil fuels.

'Renewable energy should be able to meet 85 per cent of global needs by 2050.'
IPCC (Intergovernmental Panel on Climate Change), October 2018

Looking ahead

Clean, renewable energy – such as wind, sun, wave and natural heat energy from underground – can power modern life. These clean energies do not pollute the planet. New, alternative fuels are also being developed to replace oil and gas. By switching to these cleaner sources of energy, businesses and people all over the world can shift away from fossil fuels.

As the climate emergency grows, more and more people are realising the need to leave fossil fuels in the ground. Switching to renewables is one of the most important actions individuals can take to stop climate change.

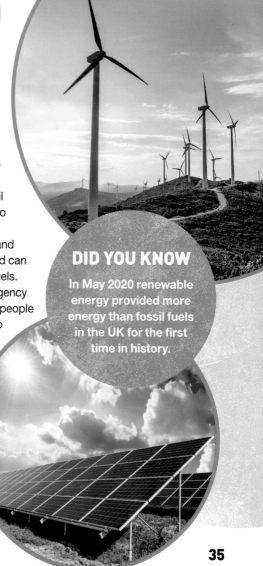

DID YOU KNOW

In May 2020 renewable energy provided more energy than fossil fuels in the UK for the first time in history.

THE BIG ISSUES
WASTE

The air, land and sea are polluted by things that are produced and thrown away by people. This waste is threatening the health of the natural world that we depend on to survive. It also takes a lot of energy to produce all the stuff that we use, and often it then travels around the world before it is sold. To reduce carbon emissions and pollution, therefore, the life cycle of everything we use must be sustainable. Where possible, it should have a positive impact on local communities and the environment.

'A truckload of clothing is wasted every second across the world.'
Ellen MacArthur Foundation report, November 2017

Challenges

Use less stuff:
Most of us buy and use more things than we need, and we throw lots of things away. If we buy less, there will be less waste.

Make things more sustainably:
The challenge is to make stuff using less energy (and renewable energy) and from materials that do not pollute or damage the environment.

Recycle, rent or upcycle:
Instead of throwing things away, we can be more creative and follow the three rs: reduce, reuse and recycle. That means mending, swapping and finding new uses for old things.

Most Preferred

Reduce

Reuse

Recycle

Recover

Dispose

Least Preferred

The life cycle of a product

This starts with the making or growing of the materials a product is made from, and then includes its manufacture, transport, use and, finally, its disposal.

Fast fashion

One of the biggest waste problems is fast fashion and throwaway clothes. At current levels, by 2050 the industry will have consumed over one-quarter of the world's carbon budget. The fashion industry's big environmental footprint is caused by:

- The use of unsustainable materials such as cotton, the growing of which uses huge amounts of fresh water.
- Plastic microfibres in clothing that are washed into the waterways and then to the sea.
- Transport of clothing around the world, which uses fossil fuels.
- Pollution in the manufacturing process, which eventually washes into the sea.
- Landfill of clothes thrown away, which generates methane, a powerful greenhouse gas.

DISCOVER MORE

Upcycling is about creatively turning something used into something new, giving it a new lease of life. Try turning an old pair of jeans into a handbag!

Looking ahead

To care for the planet and protect biodiversity, including ourselves, humans need to learn to live sustainably, especially with growing numbers of people on Earth. This means only using what we need, sharing what we have and taking care to live in harmony with the planet so future populations can also thrive and survive. So, maybe it's time to look at your wardrobe and have a rethink. Ask yourself: 'Do I really need that brand new jacket or can I share, borrow or buy from a charity shop instead?'

'Buy less. Choose well. Make it last. Quality, not quantity. Everybody's buying far too many clothes.'
Dame Vivienne Westwood (British fashion designer), September 2013

BUILDINGS

More and more people around the world are moving into cities, hoping for a better standard of life. These crowded urban spaces are mostly built from concrete – the most widely used material on Earth. However, making concrete releases gigantic amounts of carbon dioxide. Heating or cooling these buildings is also one of the biggest uses of energy on the planet. So, it follows that designing and building energy-efficient homes, schools and offices out of sustainable, efficient materials is one of the most important ways to tackle global climate change.

DID YOU KNOW?

Building like the Taipei Public Library in Taiwan, with large windows use less electricity. They can be opened so in hotter countries, there is less need for fans and air-conditioning.

Challenges

Insulate buildings:
This can reduce the amount of energy that is wasted. It saves money and energy if buildings are built in a way that stops heat escaping. Another way to do this is to make buildings more airtight, for example in Passivehaus designs.

Use renewable energy:
By choosing renewable energy to heat buildings, everyone can reduce their environmental impact.

Use sustainable materials:
There are alternatives to concrete but at the moment they are expensive... Using greener building materials such as wood can reduce environmental impact.

The passivehaus

A German-inspired housing system that requires buildings to have a super low environmental impact.
Passivehaus homes are airtight, which means they stay warm without the need for much heating.

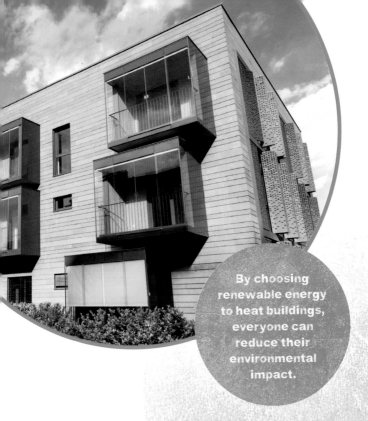

By choosing renewable energy to heat buildings, everyone can reduce their environmental impact.

'The best friend on Earth of man is the tree. When we use the tree respectfully and economically, we have one of the greatest resources on the Earth.'
Frank Lloyd Wright, architect

Looking ahead

From grass roofs to extra-thick insulation, low-energy lighting and exciting new building materials, designers, architects and engineers are coming up with new ideas for green buildings with a smaller impact on the environment. If these homes and offices were built in urban areas where walking and cycling were encouraged and where there were plenty of green spaces, living in cities could be sustainable, clean and green.

DISCOVER MORE

Green roofs and living walls covered in plants create habitats for wildlife like insects, birds and important pollinating bees.

THE BIG ISSUES
EDUCATION

There is growing evidence showing that educating girls helps to stop climate change. In fact, global investigations into solutions to climate change put educating girls and family planning in the top ten. The evidence is clear: sending more girls to school is one of the best ways to reduce carbon emissions with a growing world population of 7.7 billion people. It also improves the lives of girls and women, and the health and well-being of their families.

'Though we loved school, we hadn't realized how important education was until the Taliban tried to stop us. Going to school, reading and doing our homework wasn't just a way of passing time, it was our future.'
Malala Yousafzai, from her book *I am Malala*

Challenges

Education:

This gives girls and women the confidence to make choices about whether or not to marry. It also enables them to be stronger members of the community and therefore to be less vulnerable. Educated women have the knowledge they need to raise healthier families and to be wiser and more productive farmers.

Voluntary family planning:

This gives girls and women access to contraception and health planning, which leads to smaller, planned families as well as better awareness of hygiene and access to sanitary products.

Gender equality:

This gives women and men the same rights, without unfair discrimination.

What is period poverty?

This is something that happens when girls do not have access to sanitary products, hygienic spaces and health advice. It makes it hard for them to manage their periods with dignity.

'Data from 68 countries indicates that a woman's education is a key factor in determining a child's survival.'
UNWomen (a global champion for gender equality), 2012

'263 million children do not go to school, and twice as many girls as boys will never even start school.'
ActionAid UK, November 2019

'When 130 million girls are unable to become engineers or journalists or CEOs because education is out of their reach, our world misses out on trillions of dollars.'
Malala Yousafzai (winner of the 2014 Nobel Peace Prize), July 2018

'Educating girls lays a foundation for vibrant lives for girls and women, their families, and their communities. It is also one of the most powerful levers available for avoiding emissions by curbing population growth.'
Paul Hawken, Project Drawdown (a global research organisation that identifies, analyses and shares solutions to climate change)

Looking ahead

Giving education, hope and opportunities to the 130 million girls who are not currently in school will help to tackle gender equality and literally help protect our planet. Women who have completed secondary education are more likely to work and earn twice as much as females with no schooling. This brings important income into families and communities facing poverty and hunger.

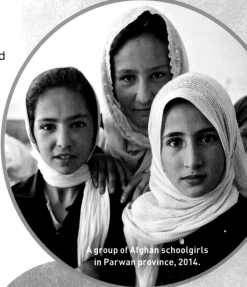

A group of Afghan schoolgirls in Parwan province, 2014.

DISCOVER MORE

Climate change affects girls and women more... Find out why at www.globalcitizen.org

THE BIG ISSUES
PLASTIC

Plastic is an incredible material that has made modern life possible. From straws and bottles to cutlery, bags and packing, plastic plays a big role in most people's lives. But the problem of plastic has now been revealed … it doesn't break down completely. This means that all the plastic that has ever been made still exists on Earth. Some breaks down into tiny micro plastics less than 5mm (1/5in) across but it never disappears. Instead, it stays in the environment, and it is damaging habitats, causing health problems for animals, including humans, and is killing marine life. Plastic is polluting the planet.

DID YOU KNOW?

The Great Pacific Garbage Patch is a gigantic swirling island of plastic in the Pacific Ocean – it covers an area three times the size of France.

Challenges

Stop using single-use plastic:

Recycling, reducing our use of plastic and cutting out single-use plastic will make a big difference. This means saying no to disposable plastic bags, straws and bottles and instead making sure you carry tote bags and reusable drinks bottles with you.

Use alternatives to plastic:

There are already plenty of alternatives to plastic, the production of which does not damage the environment, so look out for them and make plastic-free choices when you can.

It's a blue planet

The BBC TV series *Blue Planet II*, presented by Sir David Attenborough, was watched by more than 37 million people in the UK. Following the final episode, 62 per cent of those surveyed wanted to make changes to their daily lives to reduce their impact on our oceans.

Marine species from fish to seabirds, dolphins and whales eat plastic by mistake. They get caught up in it, they eat it and micro plastics are so small that they gulp them down in seawater. No-one yet fully understands what the long term impact of micro plastics is in our oceans, but we do know it is killing many different types of marine life.

'8 million tonnes of plastic ends up in our seas (mostly coming from land), threatening marine creatures and ocean habitats.'
IUCN (International Union for Conservation of Nature)

Consumer pressure

Under pressure from ordinary people, many governments and businesses are now exploring and committing to plastic-free solutions. With exciting ideas and products, like bamboo straws and going back to paper bags for fruit and vegetables, it is possible to significantly cut down the amount of plastic we use and therefore reduce plastic pollution. New technologies and inventions are proving that it will be possible to live a more plastic-free life … and so help to protect the planet.

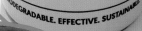

51

GET INSPIRED

Choose whose footsteps you would like to step into on your journey to becoming an eco warrior.

WORLD CHANGERS

Eco warriors are in awe of life on Earth and take action to understand and protect this precious planet. Some have completely changed our view of the world around us. They have used solid scientific evidence to explain our place on Earth and show how humans are upsetting the balance of nature. But they have also proved that with courage, conviction and character, it is possible to change this world for the better. They have given us hope. See who fills you with the greatest inspiration to protect our planet.

'The more clearly we can focus our attention on the wonders and realities of the universe about us, the less taste we shall have for destruction.'
Rachel Carson, scientist and conservationist

Charles Darwin
Changed the way we see the world

On 2 October 1836, 22-year-old Charles Darwin returned from his round-the-world voyage on HMS *Beagle* with a mountain of specimens and his head buzzing with ideas about the natural world. He then spent decades gathering evidence to understand life on Earth. Darwin lived in the 19th century, when many Europeans believed that everything on Earth was created all at once. However, like a few other scientists at the time, Darwin challenged this idea. From his meticulous scientific studies he showed that all living things, including people, evolved from a common ancestor. This is the Theory of Evolution by Natural Selection, which he finally explained in *On the Origin of Species*, the book he published in 1859. Darwin's work revolutionised our understanding of the natural world and our place in it.

DISCOVER MORE

Read Darwin's *The Origin of Species* or *The Story of Life: a first book on evolution* by Catherine Barr.

Rachel Carson
Kick-starting the revolution

Rachel was a scientist who loved the sea and writing about it. But one day she noticed that the natural world all around her was much quieter than ever before... She discovered that new chemicals used to control pests were poisoning wildlife. They were building up in the food chain and animals were dying. She wrote her discoveries down in a book called *Silent Spring*, which was published in 1962. At first, lots of people refused to believe her but eventually her evidence led to some of these poisonous chemicals being banned. Rachel inspired people to care about the natural world – and to fight to protect it. She played an important role in starting the global environmental movement.

DISCOVER MORE

Read Rachel's book *Silent Spring*, or *Spring after Spring* by Stephanie Roth Sisson – a picture book about Rachel Carson's life.

Dame Jane Goodall
Understanding our primate family

Jane had a favourite chimpanzee toy as a child and dreamed of one day living in Africa so she could watch and write about animals. She was encouraged by her mother to fulfil her dreams and has dedicated her life to studying wild chimpanzees. She famously discovered that these primates, with whom we share 98 per cent of our DNA, used tools and are more similar to humans that we ever imagined. Today, Jane Goodall campaigns around the world to save this extraordinary species, our primate family, from extinction.

DISCOVER MORE

www.janegoodall.org to explore Jane Goodall's work and campaigns or watch the National Geographic film *Jane* on Netflix.

Sir David Attenborough
Presenting nature to the world

By revealing the dazzling details as well as the big picture of the natural world, Sir David Attenborough has inspired people of all ages to marvel at our blue planet. He has shared his infectious enthusiasm and love of nature with TV audiences all over the world. Most recently, he has shared his deep concern about the consequences of the impact of humans on the planet. His words have sparked global action on plastic pollution and climate change.

DISCOVER MORE

Watch *Blue Planet* or any of the many other documentaries that Sir David Attenborough has presented about the natural world.

Greta Thunberg
Addressing the climate emergency

When she first sat alone outside the Swedish Parliament on 20 August 2018 with a banner protesting climate change, Swedish schoolgirl Greta Thunberg had no idea of the global movement she was about to inspire. She was determined to make a difference, and she has. She has since addressed global leaders and inspired young people around the globe to rise up and make their voices heard in the school #ClimateStrike movement – demanding that all of us recognise and act to address the climate emergency on planet Earth.

DISCOVER MORE

Read one of many books about Greta Thunberg and be inspired by her speeches, which can be found on YouTube.

GET INSPIRED
CAMPAIGNERS

Around the globe, there are people who care so deeply about the natural world that they have taken amazing initiatives to help save the planet. These environmental leaders have been bold, courageous and committed. Their actions as well as their words inspire other people to get involved and make long-lasting positive change.

'I would tell most young people that in life you can go through many difficulties, but if you know what you want to do, if you can focus, and work, then in the end, you will end up doing it. No matter what happens, if you don't give up, you will still succeed.'
William Kamkwamba, inventor and author

William Kamkwamba
Harnessing the power of wind

William was born into a poor family in Malawi in Africa in 1987. His family was unable to afford to send him to school. Despite this, when his community was threatened by drought, William found books in the school library that helped him understand the power and potential of the wind, and he had an inspired idea of how to bring water to the dying crops. William persuaded his community, desperate for food as crops failed to grow without rain, to build a windmill he designed, which created electricity to pump water up out of the ground to irrigate the crops. His brilliant, brave idea saved the village from famine. Today his Malawi-based organisation Moving Windmills inspires solutions that change people's lives.

DISCOVER MORE

Read the book *The Boy Who Harnessed the Wind* by William Kamkwamba or watch the film of the same name.

Inna Modja
Singer presenting the Great Green Wall

The Great Green Wall is an epic Africa-led ambition to plant a wall of trees 8,000km (5,000 miles) long across Africa. This gigantic project to reforest degraded lands across the continent has been brought to world attention by Inna Modja, a popular Malian singer and climate change activist, who presents a global, award-winning film. In it, she shows how communities across 11 countries will create the largest living structure on the planet.

DISCOVER MORE

Watch *The Great Green Wall* trailer on YouTube.

Irving Stowe
Inspiring Greenpeace

Greenpeace, one of the first global organisations to campaign to save the planet, was founded by a small group of people including Irving Stowe in 1970. Their aim was to 'bear witness' to the testing of the world's most powerful bomb in the Pacific Ocean, a bold and brave act in a tiny boat. They demanded peace on Earth and shocked the world by putting the spotlight on this deadly blast. Their direct action hit the headlines and a new, dynamic global protest movement was born. Today, Greenpeace has almost 2.8 million members, three ocean-going ships and continues to effectively campaign to protect planet Earth.

DISCOVER MORE

See what Greenpeace is doing now at www.greenpeace.org.

RAINBOW WARRIOR

GREENPEACE

Omari McQueen
The youngest vegan chef

When he was seven, Omari's mum became sick. So that Omari could help out in the family, his dad, who worked late, taught him to cook. He loved it. Cooking became his passion and after watching a film about how badly many animals are treated in the meat industry, he became a vegan. He posted a video on YouTube of himself making a vegan pizza, which sparked an award-winning career as a Caribbean vegan chef and restaurant owner. He even has his own brand of vegan products, Dipalicious!

TRY OUR NEWEST FLAVOR

DIPALICIOUS

EAT WELL
LIVE WELL

At Dipalicious we provide a selection of healthy vegan snacks for everyone to enjoy.

Shop Now

Created By 11 Year Old
Omari McQueen

DISCOVER MORE

Find Omari on Instagram @Dipaliciousltd or check out his cooking videos on YouTube.

Majora Carter
Turning cities green

Majora was walking her dog in the Bronx, New York, by a riverbank so full of rubbish that it was impossible to see the river. When Majora's dog dived through the rubbish towards the water, she followed and it gave her an idea. She became determined to rescue and restore green nature to this waterside, opening it up for families and children in the city to enjoy. She therefore began to campaign, raising awareness of the importance of nature in an urban environment. She dreamed of fresh grass, trees, flowers, water and space. Her enthusiasm spread and money followed. So, working with others, she was able to fulfil her dream. Majora has now worked on many similar projects in other places, bringing nature into cities for everyone to enjoy.

DISCOVER MORE

Watch Majora's TED Talk, *Greening the Ghetto* on YouTube.

GET INSPIRED
ACTIVISTS

Sometimes people who make a difference are ordinary people who become extraordinary. They make the world a better place by taking action that shows how the world can be a better place. Their bold vision and enthusiasm encourages others to support their eco campaigns, joined in global movements for change. When people see positive change in action, this helps to spread the word and inspire collective action.

'We cannot tire or give up. We owe it to the present and future generations of all species to rise up and walk!'
Wangari Maathai, Nobel Peace prize winner, founder of the Green Belt Movement in Africa

Extinction Rebellion
A global rebellion to save the planet

Extinction Rebellion is a do-it-together movement created by lots of people around the world, without one leader. Groups of people have united around the belief that: 'We are facing an unprecedented global emergency. Life on Earth is in crisis: scientists agree we have entered a period of abrupt climate breakdown, and we are in the midst of a mass extinction of our own making'. Across the world, people are joining this non-violent 'disruptive' action for change. This eco-rebellion has three demands in the UK: 1. That the Government tells the truth and declares a climate and ecological emergency 2. That the Government acts now to halt biodiversity loss and reduce greenhouse gas emissions to net zero by 2025 and 3. That the Government create and be led by the decisions of a 'Citizens' Assembly' on climate and ecological justice.

DISCOVER MORE

Find out what a 'Citizen's Assembly' is, at www.rebellion.earth

Augustine Oti Yeboah
Inspiring children to save pangolins

Augustine works in the University of Energy and Natural Resources in Ghana, Africa but much of his time is spent campaigning to raise awareness of the need for the conservation of pangolins. These strange-looking, scaly creatures are the most trafficked animals in the world. They are killed for their meat and their scales, which are used illegally in traditional medicines. Their survival is also threatened by habitat loss. Augustine works tirelessly with schools, raising awareness of the value of these extraordinary, rare forest animals. His environmental awareness team also helps local communities to explore ecotourism based on the pangolin and other species – so local people understand why it's important to conserve pangolins and visitors are able to discover these shy, endangered animals.

Melati and Isabel Wijsen
Fighting plastic bags together

Inspired by a lesson at school in Bali on inspiring people, sisters Melati and Isabel wondered what they could do to stop plastic pollution. These young eco entrepreneurs, aged just 11 and 12, started ByeByePlasticBags, a company that inspires teams of young people across the world to take action to deal with plastic. They encourage businesses to find alternatives to plastic bags, help clean up waterways and have created an education booklet to raise awareness of the plastic problem.

DISCOVER MORE

Look up their website and discover groups all over the world following their example to cut plastic pollution: www.byebyeplasticbags.org.

CHECK YOUR FACTS

Your words, conversations and ideas can have a powerful impact if they are supported by facts, so double-check your information.

WHAT IS A FACT?

To be successful in your mission to bring about change, you must be sure of the facts. With rigorous research, you can gain the knowledge and information you need to be respected, have integrity and convince others. But, most importantly, your facts have to be accurate and true.

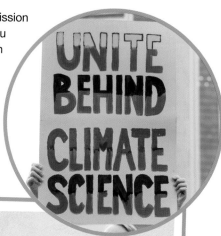

Eco glossary

Fact Something that is definitely true. A fact has been proved to be true with information.

Opinion A belief that is not necessarily based on facts or information.

Integrity The quality of being honest and having strong moral principles that you refuse to change.

Rigorous To carefully look at or consider every part of something to make certain it is correct or safe.

Ten facts to fire up an eco warrior

1
Since 1980, greenhouse gas emissions have doubled.

2
Nearly 200 million people depend on coral reefs for protection against storm surge and waves.

4
6 billion tonnes of fish and seafood have been taken from the world's oceans since 1950.

3
Almost 20% of the Amazon has disappeared in just 50 years.

5
At least 680 vertebrate species have been driven to extinction in the last 400 years.

Discover more:
Look up WWF's latest Living Planet Report to discover more facts about our natural world.

9
Over the past 50 years our Ecological Footprint has increased by about 190%

6
One million species are now threatened with extinction.

8
Marine plastic pollution has increased tenfold since 1980.

7
Since 1970, the global human population has more than doubled (from 3.7 to 7.7 billion).

10
90% of seabirds are estimated to have fragments of plastic in their stomach.

THE EVIDENCE

There are different kinds of evidence … from eyewitness accounts when you see something first hand to scientific evidence based on accurate measurements, observations and analysis. Evidence can be weak or strong but it can reliably prove the truth with facts and information.

What is scientific evidence?

This is information that is gathered by scientific research. It is based on the collection of accurate, reliable information over time. It must be done ethically (not harming any person's human rights) and safely. This information can be collected and studied in a laboratory or outside in nature, or both. Most importantly, it must be 'peer reviewed'. This is the process that turns research into evidence. It involves written research reports being critically examined by other scientists, who decide whether the data, research methods and conclusions are accurate and can therefore be published.

One example of an organisation that does a lot of scientific research is the IPCC (Intergovernmental Panel on Climate Change). It studies the world's climate using 2,000 scientists working in 80 countries.

What is bearing witness?

This term means watching something happen with your own eyes – and telling and showing the world what you have seen. By truthfully recording what you see and sharing it online or in the press, bearing witness can be a powerful, non-scientific way to bring about positive change.

The organisation Greenpeace is famous for bearing witness to help stop whaling. In tiny inflatable boats, Greenpeace activists filmed the whalers who were harpooning and killing whales. These pictures of the gigantic whaling ship and Greenpeace's tiny boat, bearing a 'Stop Whaling' banner, were splashed across newspapers and TVs around the world. They shocked and inspired many people to join this international campaign to stop whaling and save the planet's biodiversity.

July, 2013. Greenpeace activists drive on a small rubber boat with a banner reading 'Stop whaling' in front of a large container ship laden with whale meat.

STOP WHALING!

GREENPEACE

WHO TO TRUST?

There is a lot of fake news around today. This is news that isn't true. It is based on inaccurate and untruthful information. Many people believe fake news because they do not know it is not true or perhaps because it supports their existing beliefs. Luckily, there are some things you can do to work out whether or not you can trust the information you see or hear.

Check your facts

Your words, conversations and ideas can have a powerful impact if they are supported by the truth … so always double-check your facts.

'Progress is impossible without change, and those who cannot change their minds cannot change anything.'

George Bernard Shaw, author and activist

What's the source?

Here are four helpful steps
recommended by the UK National
Literacy Trust for spotting fake
news. Check out NewsWise
with tips and activities for families
to learn about news together.
www.literacytrust.org.uk/
programmes/news-wise.

STOP	If you hear something you're not sure about, stop and think about it before you decide whether or not you believe it.
QUESTION	How does the story make you feel? Does the story worry you or challenge your beliefs?
CHECK	Who wrote the story or gave you the information? Does it use official sources, such as ones from a government or an internationally respected news source, or organisation? Are other sources supporting the same news? Does it quote experts working for reputable organisations? You can check the facts yourself at www.fullfact.org.
DECIDE	If you decide to trust the source, perhaps you will share the information and start a conversation ... or even a debate!

CHECK YOUR FACTS
RELIABLE SOURCES

There are lots of different well-respected national and international organisations who provide evidence of the damage we are causing the natural world. Explore these websites to find powerful facts that you can use to start a conversation, debate or a chat at home around the kitchen table.

Friends of the Earth (FoE)
The largest grassroots environmental campaigning community in the UK. It works with local groups, experts, business leaders and politicians.
www.friendsoftheearth.uk

Greenpeace International
A global environmental organisation operating in over 55 countries.
www.greenpeace.org

International Union for Conservation of Nature
The Red List is a global directory of 116,000 species, which are assessed for their conservation status by 8,000 scientists around the world.
www.IUCNredlist.org

SCIENCE
KNOWS NO COUNTRY
BECAUSE KNOWLEDGE
BELONGS TO HUMANITY
AND IS THE TORCH WHICH
ILLUMINATES THE WORLD
~ LOUIS PASTEUR

The Intergovernmental Panel on Climate Change
The United Nations body responsible for assessing science related to climate change. www.IPCC.ch

Marine Conservation Society (MCS)
Working for the protection of seas, shores and wildlife in the UK. www.MCSUK.org

Rewilding Europe
Rewilding spaces for wildlife and people. www.rewildingeurope.com

Royal Society for the Protection of Birds (RSPB)
The largest conservation charity in the UK, which works to create bigger, better, joined-up spaces to save wildlife and birds. www.rspb.org.uk

TRAFFIC
An organisation working to combat the illegal global trade in wild animals and plants. www.traffic.org

United Nations (UN)
Countries work together as United Nations to take action on peace and security, climate change, sustainable development, human rights, disarmament, terrorism, humanitarian and health emergencies and more. www.un.org

WasteAid
Fighting poverty, pollution and climate change. www.wasteaid.org

Water Aid
Campaigning for clean water, decent toilets and good hygiene. www.wateraid.co.uk

World Health Organization
Building a better, healthier future for people all over the world. www.who.int

World Wide Fund for Nature
International organisation working to stop the destruction of nature and help it recover. www.wwf.org.uk

SKILL UP

If you want to be an eco warrior you need all sorts of different skills to succeed ... discover if you have what it takes to change the world.

HOW TO INSPIRE

E co warriors can use a whole range of skills to have an impact and inspire positive change. Here are just a few to think about. Are you curious? Do you listen? Are you brave? Can you make people laugh? Find out if you can change the world.

Eco warriors are CURIOUS

If you are curious, you are inquisitive and interested in the world around you. You want to learn things. Curious children ask questions and listen because they really want to know the answers (short, clear ones are best).

'I think, at a child's birth, if a mother could ask a fairy godmother to endow it with the most useful gift, that gift would be curiosity.'

Eleanor Roosevelt (American diplomat, activist and Presidential First Lady)

Eco warriors gather KNOWLEDGE

To campaign, you need facts, information and skills – this knowledge will help you to persuade others to join your cause.

'Wisdom is not a product of schooling but of the lifelong attempt to acquire it.'

Albert Einstein (German-American physicist)

Eco warriors must UNDERSTAND

If you understand the facts and information that you have, you are more likely to use the information wisely and be better able to share your knowledge with other people.

'The improvement of understanding is for two ends: first, our own increase of knowledge; secondly, to enable us to deliver that knowledge to others.'

John Locke (English philosopher and physician)

Eco warriors are filled with PASSION

If you really want to do something and you are filled with enthusiasm, you have a powerful feeling called passion. This strong emotion will inspire you to act!

'Passion is energy. Feel the power that comes from focusing on something that excites you.'

Oprah Winfrey (American talk show host)

Eco warriors use HUMOUR

Humour is making someone laugh or at least bringing a smile to their face – even in sad or really challenging situations. Humour can break down barriers and help people to understand each other.

'A sense of humor is part of the art of leadership, of getting along with people, of getting things done.'

**Dwight D. Eisenhower
(34th President
of America)**

Eco warriors tell GOOD STORIES

One of the best ways of all to save the planet is to tell a story, because everyone loves a story – and listens. If you gather your facts and find examples that excite and interest people, you can grab their attention.

A story can be written in a book or it can be told. Stories help because they paint pictures in your mind. They have the power to help you imagine, dream, hope and inspire. Try it!

Tell someone why you care about the planet. What made you get involved and want to help change the world? Did it happen one day or by surprise or because of something you saw or something someone said? Try and remember and tell your story… Or write it down and share it with your class and family.

'Stories make you think and dream; books make you want to ask questions.'
Sir Michael Morpurgo (English book author, poet and playwright), Children's Laureate 2003–05

Eco warriors have COURAGE

Being an eco warrior takes courage because sometimes you have to be brave. You may need to face an uncomfortable situation and be bold to succeed!

'Your time is limited, so don't waste it living someone else's life… And most important, have the courage to follow your heart and intuition.'

**Steve Jobs (former Apple CEO),
Stanford University speech 2005**

Eco warriors spread EMPATHY

Without empathy you cannot succeed. Empathy is the ability to understand and share someone else's feelings from their point of view. Imagine you are standing in their shoes.

'When you start to develop your powers of empathy and imagination, the whole world opens up to you.'

Susan Sarandon (activist and actress)

Eco warriors spread KINDNESS

Being kind is about caring about other people. It is about being generous and friendly. Kindness is catching… If you are kind to people, it will make you and them (and lots of other people) feel happier.

'Sometimes it takes only one act of kindness and caring to change a person's life.'

Jackie Chan (Hong Kong film director)

Eco warriors are DETERMINED

To succeed, you need to be determined, which means you need to be sure about what you want to do and stick to your goals, however difficult they may be. Determination is a strong, positive feeling.

'The best way to not feel hopeless is to get up and do something. Don't wait for good things to happen to you. If you go out and make some good things happen, you will fill the world with hope, you will fill yourself with hope.'

Barack Obama (44th President of America)

ASK QUESTIONS

You don't have to be a grown-up to help save the planet. Teenager Greta Thunberg and millions of other children around the world (perhaps you too?) have shown grown-ups that they care about the planet and that together we can all make a bigger difference – and change the world.

Find out:

➡ Who or what is causing the problem?

➡ Where in the world is the problem?

➡ Which are the organisations and experts leading campaigns for change?

➡ How can the problem be solved?

➡ What can you do to help?

Using words

Whether you are writing to your head teacher to ask if your school can please raise money to help save bees, or to your local MP to vote to save green spaces in your town, writing letters or sending emails can make a big impact. It's important to send them to the person who can make the decisions, so your words are not wasted.

Once you have decided what really inspires you – whether it's reducing plastic pollution or saving polar bears – find out some facts. Visit a library to find books on the subjects you are interested in and research them properly. Try asking your teachers, parents and friends whether they can help you find out more information.

But how you make a difference depends on who you are and what you are good at. You might be great at remembering fantastic facts that persuade your friends and family to join in, you might enjoy chanting on a march, or you might rather sit quietly and write letters to challenge your MP. Or perhaps you'd like to explore opportunities to volunteer with a charity or be brave and organise a school assembly.

READ ABOUT IT

To discover the story of the issue you are interested in, it's a good idea to get lost in a book or hang out in the library. Reading non-fiction picture books and chapter books will really help you get to grips with the subject you are interested in and answer your questions.

Explore the library catalogue and ask for books that you would like to read, if they are not already on the shelves. You could also make sure that this book is in the catalogue, to help other eco warriors get started too!

But of course you can also look safely online, listen to the radio, find podcasts and watch TV programmes and films. There are lots of different ways of finding information that can help you understand what you are interested in. But books are always a good place to start this exciting information journey.

Actions

➥ Ask for books for birthdays and Christmas.
➥ Search for books in your local charity shops.
➥ Borrow books from friends.
➥ Join a book club at school or suggest one if none exist.
➥ Buy second-hand books online.

TALK ABOUT IT

Now that you understand the issue and are full of facts and useful knowledge, see if you can persuade other people to help you save the world. It takes skill to explain something simply and convince other people to change their minds. To grab their attention, you'll need to talk clearly and remember some powerful facts to convince others to join your cause.

Practise your arguments by talking about your chosen issue with family and friends. See if you can answer their questions, listen to their views and learn together. If you don't know the answers to their questions, look them up so next time you're ready to make your case! Enjoy the challenge, share your thoughts and welcome debate about the issues that interest you most.

Actions

➡ You can talk, show videos or read out loud.

➡ Be ready for a debate and get ready to answer questions – have the responses up your sleeve.

➡ Show how they can make a difference and why it matters.

THE POWER OF WORDS

Words matter... If you speak clearly – with kindness, respect, enthusiasm and encouragement – you can make a positive, long-lasting difference. Remember, it's not just what you say, but how you say it that matters.

THE POWER OF WORDS
SPEAKING

Whether you are talking, writing or posting online, the way you use language to communicate will make a difference. If you are open to conversation, positive in your attitude, compassionate and clear, it is more likely that people will listen and be engaged, and you may even change their minds.

Word of mouth

From chatting in the school playground to talking in youth clubs, on the street with friends and round the kitchen table at home, talking about stuff helps to raise awareness. If you are enthusiastic, people listen and if you are full of fascinating facts and good stories, people listen even more. By talking to people you can encourage them to join you in your eco mission to save the world.

Actions

➥ Chat to your neighbours and see whether they want to help you organise a summer street party or another fun event to raise money for your campaign.

➥ Talk to your teachers to plan a 'Whale of an Assembly'. Suggest that your class runs a cake stall to raise money to support a charity that campaigns to save the whales.

➥ Gossip with your friends and plan a sponsored event (make it a lot of fun … whatever you enjoy doing most!) to raise money for your favourite endangered animal – whether it's a panda or a pangolin.

➥ See whether your school may be interested in setting up an eco warrior club. Here, you can talk about eco issues and make things from recycled materials.

➥ Try to persuade your parents and teachers to be eco friendly at school events. You could ask that people bring along their own travel cups rather than using disposable cups for tea and coffee, make sure there are different bags for different types of waste (draw posters to make it clear which is which), and avoid all single-use plastic, such as teaspoons and cracker-style toys as prizes.

THE POWER OF WORDS
WRITING

We write to express all sorts of emotions, from sadness to excitement and joy. Writing can persuade, inspire, surprise and encourage, so as an eco warrior, you need to choose your words well. From funny slogans to heart-warming letters and persuading statements, it's time to tap on your keyboard or pick up your pen.

Big pens writing big messages

To make a banner for a protest march or eco warrior event, you need a good slogan and a big piece of cardboard, or even a ripped-up old sheet (with your parents' permission…!).

You need to come up with a short, punchy phrase that says it all. It might be funny, clever or even rude! If it's good and original it might even get on the news … which will help to spread your message even further and engage even more people with your cause.

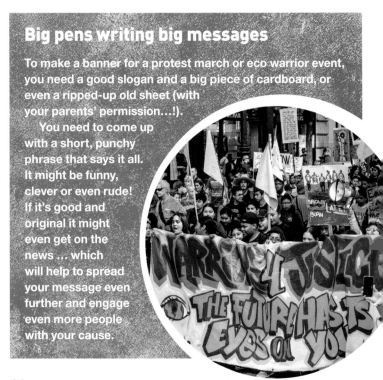

Here are some ideas for banner messages for eco protests:

CLIMATE CHANGE IS WORSE THAN HOMEWORK

THERE'S NO PLANET B

ANIMAL RIGHTS NOT WRONGS

I'M SURE THE DINOSAURS THOUGHT THEY HAD TIME TOO

SCIENCE NOT SILENCE

LIKE THE OCEANS, WE RISE

HOW DARE YOU

I'D BE IN SCHOOL IF EARTH WAS COOL

PLANET OVER PROFIT

CHANGE THE SYSTEM NOT THE CLIMATE

ONLY FOSSILS LIKE FOSSIL FUELS

THE POWER OF WORDS
LETTERS

H ave you ever written a letter? Hand-written letters used to be a really popular and easy way for people to share ideas and opinions. Now, most people send emails and share ideas online. Whichever method you choose, you can make an impact.

Social media

Whether or not you have your own phone, you will know friends and family who do. You'll also know that viral video news spreads pretty fast, especially with a hashtag # on Instagram or Twitter. It's easy to see which are the most popular. When you type them in, the number that comes up will show you how popular it is. You can explore popular eco hashtags that you can use to share your eco warrior actions and spread your news, or you can create your own!

Here are a few to look up to see what other eco warriors are up to:

#Climatestrikes   #ecowarriors   #savetheplanet
#earthday   #ecofriendly   #zerowaste

Actions

➡ **Sign a petition.** If you get 10,000 signatures, the government has to respond. For more information, check out www.petition.parliament.uk/help.

➡ **Write a letter.** You can write to anyone whose mind you would like to change. It may be the head of a big company (perhaps you want them to stop polluting the local river), your local shop (perhaps you want them to sell organic vegetables), your local council (perhaps you want them to recycle more plastic) or even your head teacher at school (perhaps you want to suggest locally sourced food for school dinners). Whoever you want to write to, the more letters they receive, the more notice they are likely to take. So get everyone else writing too!

➡ **Write an article.** If you fancy becoming a journalist one day, you might want to practise your skills. Why not write an article (or a letter) for your local newspaper or perhaps your school newsletter? This may trigger some interesting conversations and invite people to join a debate or share their views.

What is a petition?

It is a statement that people support with their signature. If lots of people sign a petition, it shows that lots of people are supporting the statement. This is then delivered to the person you are asking to make the change. This might be your local MP.

THE POWER OF WORDS
BOOKS & SONGS

Get lost in a book or hang out in the library. Whether you are writing a letter or talking to friends, accurate facts and information will be important. Reading all kinds of books – fiction and non-fiction – will help you explore the subject and issue you are interested in, and understand different perspectives.

Explore the library catalogue and ask for books that you would like to read, if they are not already on the shelves. You could also make sure that this book is in the catalogue, to help other eco warriors get started!

Protest songs and poems

Song lyrics and poetry have inspired protesters and eco warriors for generations. From John Lennon's famous song about world peace 'Imagine' to Joni Mitchell's famous 'Big Yellow Taxi', which was inspired by a car park in Hawaii, there are plenty of protest songs that will help get you in the mood to stand up and be heard.

Songs and poems are powerful ways to get messages across to lots of people… With big audiences and huge followings, they help to raise awareness of all kinds of issues, from poverty to peace and climate change.

Have a go at writing the lyrics to your own protest song. Perhaps you have a friend in a band and can persuade them to sing along? Send it to the local paper and see if they will publish your precious and powerful words!

Have a listen…

There are lots of songs about the environment and climate change. Here are just a few, old and new, that you can look up on YouTube:

'Idioteque'
by Radiohead

'The Seed'
by Aurora

'Evolutionicide'
by Spencer Maybe

'Imagine'
by John Lennon

'Who's Gonna Stand Up'
by Neil Young

'Big Yellow Taxi'
by Joni Mitchell

'Don't Go Near the Water'
by The Beach Boys

'Mercy Mercy Me'
by Marvin Gaye

TAKE ACTION

Actions can speak louder than words...
So it's time to rise up, join in and make
decisions that will help save the planet.

TAKE ACTION
GET UP & JOIN IN

Now you understand more about the issues it's time to take action. There are lots of different things you can do to join in and show your feelings or actively help with a problem – from going on marches to volunteering with a local wildlife group.

'Young people may lack experience but they also have clear sight ... They can perhaps see more clearly than the rest of us who have been around for some time. My generation is no great example for understanding – we have done terrible things. If we are not making progress with young people we are done.'

Sir David Attenborough, natural historian

Make a banner by spray painting cardboard and holding it up high.

JOIN A MARCH

If you've already been on a Climate Strike for School inspired by Greta Thunberg then you know how to march! Marching with protest banners and a popular chant is a powerful and fun way to show the world that you care, together.

Actions

➡ Make a banner by spray painting cardboard and holding it up high.

➡ Use an old bed sheet and make a big banner so your message gets noticed – you might even spot yourself on the news!

105

JUST SIT DOWN

Sitting down as a protest is one kind of non-violent direct action. This is a peaceful protest that can have a powerful impact. There are lots of examples in history of people who have refused to move in order to raise awareness, get noticed and provoke change.

Non violent direct action (NVDA) is a peaceful way to protest. Discover more at www.greenpeace.org.uk/news/six-greenpeace-non-violent-direct-actions

Actions

➤ Learn about Rosa Parks, a young black woman who refused to move from the whites-only area of a bus in South Africa.

➤ Look up 'Swampy', a young man who sat in trees in the UK to stop them from being cut down to build roads.

➤ See how Greta Thunberg began her climate campaign by sitting down every Friday outside the Swedish parliament building with a homemade banner.

You can learn plenty of new skills as a volunteer... and make lots of new friends too!

VOLUNTEER

If you are really ready to take action, you might decide to give some of your free time to help. Whether you are collecting signatures for a school petition in your lunch break or making banners for a march after school, you can be an eco warrior volunteer!

Actions

➥ Ask a charity if you can help – perhaps you can plant seeds in a community garden at weekends.
➥ Take part in a nearby 'Beach Clean' or a 'River Clean' to help clear up plastic and stop pollution.
➥ Join a wildlife club to help raise awareness and pick up eco living tips to share.

SHOPPING

Most of us buy too much stuff and much of it eventually ends up in the bin. Buying things is called consumerism and it's one of the biggest causes of environmental problems around the world. To live sustainably – that is to protect the planet for future generations – we need to buy less. Less consumption uses less of the Earth's precious resources, causing less pollution and creating less waste.

> 'Our relentless consumption is trashing the planet'
> **George Monbiot, author and journalist**

Actions

➥ **Just buy less.**
Ask: Do you really need it? Can I upcycle something I already have? Can I buy it second-hand or from a charity shop? Can I borrow it instead?

➥ **Shop sustainably.**
Ask: What's the most sustainable option? Is it made from recycled products? Does it biodegrade? Is it made of a material that requires less water, such as sustainable cotton? Is it organic?

➥ **Boycott products or whole companies who are damaging the environment.** Check out www. ethicalconsumer.org. This is a website that rates companies according to a wide range of issues, from animal welfare to pollution, climate change and environmental reporting.

Organic and sustainable products

Sustainable, organic farming causes little or no damage to the environment, using natural methods that help nurture the soil and protect the environment. Organic farmers commit to strict regulations that encourage wildlife and cut the use of pesticides and antibiotics.

TAKE ACTION
TRAVELLING

There are lots of ways to travel on long and short journeys. Some cause pollution by burning fossil fuels while others are free, clean and green. You may have a choice. If so, you can encourage and inspire friends to join you walking, cycling, catching the bus and scooting along. Can you find holidays closer to home, with no air travel and fewer car miles?

The COVID-19 pandemic may have an impact on travel around the world that could actually benefit the environment. With greater emphasis and investment in walking and cycling and less flying, there would be less pollution and healthier people and places.

Copenhagen, Denmark's capital, is one of the most bike-friendly cities in the world.

Actions

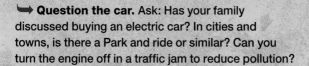

➥ **Avoid flying if possible.** Ask: Do we really need to fly? Could I carbon offset my flight?

➥ **For shorter journeys, walk or cycle … enjoy the healthy exercise!** Ask: Can I borrow or share a bike? Can I ask for one for my birthday?

➥ **Question the car.** Ask: Has your family discussed buying an electric car? In cities and towns, is there a Park and ride or similar? Can you turn the engine off in a traffic jam to reduce pollution?

➥ **Hop on the bus or the train.** Ask: Can we use buses or trains instead of the car?

What is carbon offsetting?

A system based on how much carbon dioxide is emitted by something you are doing (such as flying on holiday). You then give money to a project that will reduce carbon emissions by the same amount, such as renewable energy or forestry organisations. However, carbon offsetting is controversial. The best thing you can do is not to add to emissions in the first place.

TAKE ACTION
RECYCLING

It takes energy and resources to make stuff so it minimises your environmental impact on the planet if you buy recycled products and recycle your own things. It is now possible to recycle lots of materials – from glass and plastics to textiles, paper and card. You can also recycle by giving things you don't want any more to other people who need them – through charity shops, the online Freecycle Network or friends and family.

Throwing things away creates waste, which piles up in big holes dug underground called landfill sites. It is also dumped in the oceans. Piles of rotting rubbish create methane, a deadly greenhouse gas that contributes to climate change. As it decays, it also oozes toxic pollution. This is poisoning habitats and killing biodiversity. Most pollution in the oceans comes from land, in the form of plastics and toxics that are washing out to sea.

Actions

➡ **Buy recycled products.** Ask: What is it made from? Can I buy an alternative made of sustainable materials?

➡ **Buy biodegradable products where possible.** Ask: What will happen to this product when I have finished with it? Will it biodegrade, compost or be recycled?

➡ **Carry a recycled or reusable bag.** Ask: Why do you (shops) still offer customers plastic bags, please don't!

Start recycling

Find out where you can recycle things like crisp and biscuit packets, toothpaste tubes and toothbrushes and then spread the news. You could even organise a collection point at school – look up www.terracycle.com to find out more.

TAKE ACTION
EATING

What you eat can save the world. Intensive meat and dairy farming is responsible for as much greenhouse gas as all the direct emissions from all global transportation combined. Clearing tropical forests like the Amazon to grow soya to feed chickens and pigs in Europe, as well as for grazing for beef cattle, adds to climate change as the forest falls. By burping and farting methane, cows and other livestock like sheep also cause a big problem for the planet. Methane is a powerful greenhouse gas that makes a significant contribution to climate change.

'You cannot get through a single day without having an impact on the world around you. What you do makes a difference, and you have to decide what kind of difference you want to make.'
Jane Goodall, primatologist

Actions

➡ **Cut down on meat.** Ask: What can I eat on my non-meat days?

➡ **Be plant-based.** Ask: What can I eat instead of meat?

➡ **Explore options.** Ask: What's the difference between a vegan, vegetarian, pescatarian, flexitarian and an omnivore?

Animal welfare

Worldwide, factory farming keeps animals in miserable conditions. This intensive industry is a huge cause of animal cruelty on Earth, but it's not just about animal welfare, scientists and organisations campaigning against factory farming show how this way of farming threatens habitats, wildlife and resources. Eating local, free range produce means you are helping farmers who look after the welfare of their animals.

TAKE ACTION
AT HOME

At home, you use lots of different products to wash your clothes and yourself, clean your house, cook, relax and generally exist. Whether you're helping to do the washing up, brushing your teeth or choosing clothes to buy, everything you do has an effect on the planet. The production of some products has a big negative impact in terms of energy and water use, air miles, and toxic or unsustainable ingredients. By comparison, truly 'ethical' products have a powerful positive impact by, for example, supporting Fairtrade. Others use sustainably produced ingredients, which are made locally by local communities and businesses without needing air miles or transport that involve fossil fuels.

When you buy things, look on the labels, read the ingredients and ask questions that will help you discover greener alternatives.

Actions

➡ Check WWF's Palm Oil Buyers Scorecard and avoid companies who are not committed to 100 per cent deforestation-free palm oil in their products.

➡ Check www.ethicalconsumer. org online to find the greener brands.

➡ Find local sustainable businesses that you can support by buying their products.

➡ Buy beauty products that don't contain toxic or unsustainable ingredients, such as palm oil, and find out from www.PETA.org if they have been tested on animals.

➡ Use bars of soap and even shampoo bars instead of buying products in plastic bottles. Or take your existing bottles along to a refill shop and reuse the same bottle over and over again.

What is Fairtrade?

A scheme that fights for better prices, decent working conditions, local sustainability and fair terms of trade for farmers and workers in the developing world.

FAIRTRADE®

TAKE ACTION
OUTSIDE

The natural world is not just nice and green to look at – we need it for the air we breathe, the food we eat, the clean water we drink and wash with to keep us healthy, the materials we use for energy and medicine, and to balance our climate. Trees play a very important role in nature. As well as providing habitats for wildlife and timber for people, their roots anchor the soil, preventing flooding. They also create oxygen and suck polluting carbon dioxide gas out of the air. So, they are very important in reducing the impact of climate change. Of course, nature also provides green spaces, incredible wilderness and beauty that we can explore, play in, find peace in and enjoy.

'A nation that destroys its soils destroys itself. Forests are the lungs of our land, purifying the air and giving fresh strength to our people.'
Franklin D. Roosevelt, 32nd President of America

Actions

➡ **Plant a tree.** Planting billions of trees is one of the best ways to tackle the climate crisis. Go to www.woodlandtrust.org.uk to Pledge to Plant a Tree to Save the World. You can also use a search engine called Ecosia. For every 45 or so searches you make, they plant one tree!

➡ **Join a river or a beach clean-up.** Help collect plastic and other rubbish that has found its way into our waterways and oceans.

➡ **Plant a wildlife garden that encourages and helps bees.** Bee populations are declining due to pesticide use. This is bad because these buzzing insects are critical for pollination, which in turn is essential for growing our food and the health of our natural world.

➡ **Spend time outside.** Go for a walk and look around you. What can you see? Climb a tree or a mountain and enjoy the fresh air and the view.

TAKE ACTION
KEEP LEARNING

The first step to doing something is wanting to do it. This inspiration can come from listening to someone live or on the radio, seeing a film, watching TV, reading a book or having a conversation. It all starts with discovering knowledge and information that fills you with wonder, outrage, shock or fascination. If you feel strongly, you will be inspired to take action. With reliable information from trusted sources, you will have the power to persuade people to join you – and make a bigger impact.

'I am only one, but I am one. I cannot do everything; but I can do something. And I will not let what I cannot do interfere with what I can do.'
Edward Everett Hale, American author

Discovering new ideas

There are many different, interesting ways to learn. From visiting museums and exhibitions to talking to family and friends. But one exciting way to discover new things is to listen to podcasts and watch TED education talks online. TED talks are free online presentations by experts about exciting new ideas. People giving TED talks are passionate about what they do and good at communicating – so they are easy and interesting to listen to: www.ted.com.

Actions

➥ Visit the library and gather books.

➥ Borrow books at school.

➥ Listen to the radio and watch informative TV programmes.

➥ Ask an expert.

➥ Find organisations working on the issues you are interested in. Ask: Are these organisations reliable and trustworthy?

LOCAL TO GLOBAL

As an eco warrior, you can inspire others to join you to make a difference and provoke positive change, both in your neighbourhood and in the wider world.

START SMALL

So now you have the tools and the ideas, and you really want to make a difference. If you follow in the footsteps of eco warrior Greta Thunberg, you can start local and might end up with a global audience! Remember, you can make a huge impact by starting your own campaign among your own local friends and family.

Ask other people what they think and swap facts and ideas.

Friends and family

➡ **Start a conversation online.** Vlog, blog, make videos on what you're doing to reduce your own carbon footprint, and upload them. Make sure you follow internet guidelines for staying safe.

➡ **Challenge your friends to a debate.** Use your skills to persuade people and to try to win an argument. Can you convince someone to change their mind? Perhaps you can start a school debating club?

➡ **Go it alone.** Inspire others to copy your actions by taking the lead... Eat less meat, stop using plastic bags, buy your clothes from charity shops, use the library and recycle.

Community

➥ **Put up a poster.** Make a poster asking for help and put it up at school or in your local shop. You might gather a crowd to raise money or organise an event like a litter pick or a local river clean-up.

➥ **Write to the paper.** Test your journalism skills and write to your local paper to raise awareness of the eco issues that you feel are affecting your local community.

➥ **Celebrate with a street party.** Talk to your neighbours and see if they'll agree to help organise a plastic-free party to raise awareness and demand change.

Regional

➥ **Find out what your MP's voting record is on environmental issues.** Use www.mysociety.org or www.theyworkforyou.com to find out and if they are not doing enough, write a polite letter to ask for action for change.

➥ **Make good friends.** Discover who else cares about your eco issue in your area. Are there local youth groups whose meetings or events you could join, or organisations and people who have gathered useful information?

➥ **Discover who's in charge.** If it's a local environmental problem, get stuck into some research to find out whether a business or the council are causing the problem – they may help to solve it in the end!

GO FURTHER

As well as getting involved in local issues you can go further. You can join an existing campaign for change and become part of an international movement. This will give you the bigger picture about the impact of eco problems on the world.

National

➡ **Make new friends.** Take part in a march or demo. These draw people from all over the country, who join together to raise awareness of an issue by making headline news.

➡ **Join an organisation.** There are lots of charities campaigning for positive change to reduce environmental impact and encourage more sustainable lifestyles. Find the one that suits you and sign up … perhaps they have regular newsletters and local groups.

➡ **Watch the news.** Every day, you can find out what other people are doing and be inspired to get involved. Whether you watch TV, keep an eye on social media or sign up to a blog, there are lots of ways to find the facts and gather information to form your own opinion on issues.

International

➡ **Get the big picture.** By reading books or watching the news, you will probably discover that lots of other people all around the world care about 'your' issue too! Be inspired by their successes, get ideas and learn from their campaigns.

➡ **Network.** Find people just like you and share ideas about how to save the world.

➡ **Save the world.** You are one of more than 7.8 billion people in the world but by spreading your message, meeting others who feel the same as you and acting together, you really can change the world.

Ask other people what they think and swap facts and ideas.

'If you give nature a chance, it recovers … if the world can get together and stop doing it, it will recover. And I am optimistic.'
Sir David Attenborough, 2018

LOOK OUT FOR THESE FANTASTIC
POCKET MANUALS

POCKET MANUAL
MYTHICAL BEASTS

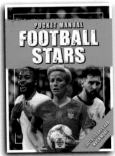

POCKET MANUAL
FOOTBALL STARS

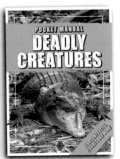

POCKET MANUAL
DEADLY CREATURES

POCKET MANUAL
SHARKS

POCKET MANUAL
KINGS & QUEENS

POCKET MANUAL
DINOSAURS

POCKET MANUAL
PREDATORS

POCKET MANUAL
SPACE

POCKET MANUAL
EXTREME CARS

www.haynes.com